Voices of the Dust Bowl

VOICES of the DUST BOWL

By Sherry Garland

Illustrated by Judith Hierstein

PELICAN PUBLISHING COMPANY
GRETNA 2012

Library of Congress Cataloging-in-Publication Data

Garland, Sherry.
  Voices of the dust bowl / by Sherry Garland ; illustrated by
Judith Hierstein.
     p. cm.
  Includes bibliographical references.
  ISBN 978-1-58980-964-2 (hardcover : alk. paper) 1. Dust Bowl
Era, 1931-1939—Juvenile literature. 2. Dust storms—Great
Plains—History—20th century—Juvenile literature. 3. Droughts—
Great Plains—History—20th century—Juvenile literature. 4. Farm-
ers—Great Plains—History—20th century—Juvenile literature. 5.
Great Plains—History—20th century—Juvenile literature. 6. Mid-
dle West—History—20th century—Juvenile literature. I. Hierstein,
Judy, ill. II. Title.
  F595.G275 2011
  973.917—dc22
                              2011002670

Printed in China
Published by Pelican Publishing Company, Inc.
1000 Burmaster Street, Gretna, Louisiana 70053

To my West Texas kinfolk, with fond memories of red earth, cotton fields, and oil wells—S.G.

To my grandchildren, Lorelei, Sagen, and Kadin Zo—J.H.

1893—Oklahoma Territory

I am an old warrior who has lived too long.
When I was a young brave, great herds of buffalo
roamed this prairie where the wind blows wild and free.

Now I see homesteaders in wagons, on horses,
in buggies, on foot, or any way they can,
rushing to grab these lands.
They will build their squatty sod houses
and pierce the earth with their plows.
Their crops will cover the earth
where once tall grasses grew.

The buffalo are gone now;
my people are dwindling to a few.
One more time before I die
I will sing a song of sorrow
for the buffalo, for my people,
and for this land I love.

1919—Western Kansas

I am a proud sodbuster
who turned this empty land
into fields of waving gold.
Naysayers called this a semi-arid plain;
the Great American Desert, they said,
a place where a farmer should beware.
But since I've been here
there has been abundant rain.

When the Great War came,
the government asked us to grow wheat
to feed the troops overseas.
The motto of America became
"Wheat will win the war!"

Getting two dollars a bushel
didn't hurt any either.

Mid-1930—Oklahoma

I'm a nervous banker
trying to gather my belongings
before I lock the doors for good.

After that bleak day last October
when the stock market crashed,
banks started closing down
all across the United States,
and the citizens who had money
in their accounts lost everything.

Angry farmers are milling around outside
with their pitchforks and shotguns
demanding I give them money
that the bank no longer has.

Once they were my friends,
but now I think it prudent
to leave by the back door.

Fall 1930—Texas Panhandle

I am a cotton picker moving field to field
with my family, trying to earn a wage.

Last spring plenty of rain fell 'round here,
and folks had walloping bumper crops.
Boll weevils weren't too bad;
had fields white as snow come this fall.

We worked day and night for the boss man,
trying to get that first bale to the gin.
But the price of cotton fell to six cents a pound,
so we pickers got paid next to nothing
for all our sweat and toil.

Wheat farmers are hit just as bad—
their price dropped to twenty-four cents a bushel.
Silos are still filled up with last year's unsold grain;
new wheat is dumped on the ground, worthless.

I heard farmers say they will have to plow up more land
'cause they aren't making enough to pay their bills.

Ain't nothing great 'bout this depression.

Fall 1932—Southeastern Colorado

I'm an ornery old cowpoke
who used to work on the XIT Ranch
down in Texas 'fore the owners sold the land
to eager nesters who tore up the soil.

Now we're deep in a drought;
hasn't rained enough to fill a thimble
for nigh over a year.
Crops withered and died this summer,
leaving the plowed fields empty and bare,
with tumbleweeds racing by.

With no roots to hold down the soil,
the prairie wind is picking it up
and blowing it to Kingdom Come.

I say this land was meant for grazing, not farming,
but nobody wants to listen to an old cowboy like me.

1933—Texas

I am Bonnie Parker
here with my sweetheart, Clyde,
and my Tommy gun in tow,
moving across this dusty land
in our latest stolen Ford V-8
looking for a bank to rob.

Times are mighty bleak.
Banks are foreclosing on farmers
who can't pay back their loans
for equipment and seeds.

It's a sad sight seeing a bank
auctioning off all a man's worldly goods
on the steps of the courthouse.

No wonder folks around here
cheer us on when we pass by.
Nobody loves a bank.

1933—Northeastern New Mexico

I am a schoolmarm
here on the Southern Plains.

This horrid drought shows no end and
dusters are getting worse each year.

Today a storm rolled up so fast
I didn't have time to send the children home.
I passed out pieces of cloth
soaked in the water bucket.
The children placed them over their faces
to help keep out the dust.

The roaring wind broke windowpanes
and stripped the paint off the boards.
The gray powder crept under the doors
and through the cracks.

I can still hear the sound of coughing children
when I try to sleep at night.

1934—Southern Nebraska

I am a farmer's wife in this desolate land
of nothing but wind and dust and heat.

Every meal I cook is full of grit;
every piece of furniture, every inch of floor
in our old dwelling is covered in dust.

When a storm hits, the children and I
hang wet blankets and wet sheets
over the doors and over the windows.
We jam pieces of cloth in every crack.
The heat and stifling air are unbearable,
yet still the powder gets in.

When the storm is over,
the doors are blocked by piles of dust.
The fences have vanished under huge drifts.
We sweep bucket loads of dust
out the door, knowing full well
that it will be back inside
with the next storm.

1935—Kansas

I am a nurse at this makeshift hospital
whose beds are overflowing with those
afflicted with "dust pneumonia."

I saw the Red Cross handing out masks
to children, but even that does not stop
the fine powder from getting into the nose,
into the lungs, and into the stomach.

Some patients are here because of heat strokes,
for the temperatures soar every summer—
all the way up to 120 degrees sometimes.

Every day I see mothers tend their dying babes,
helplessly watching the small bodies struggle for air,
cough up dirt and blood, then go still.

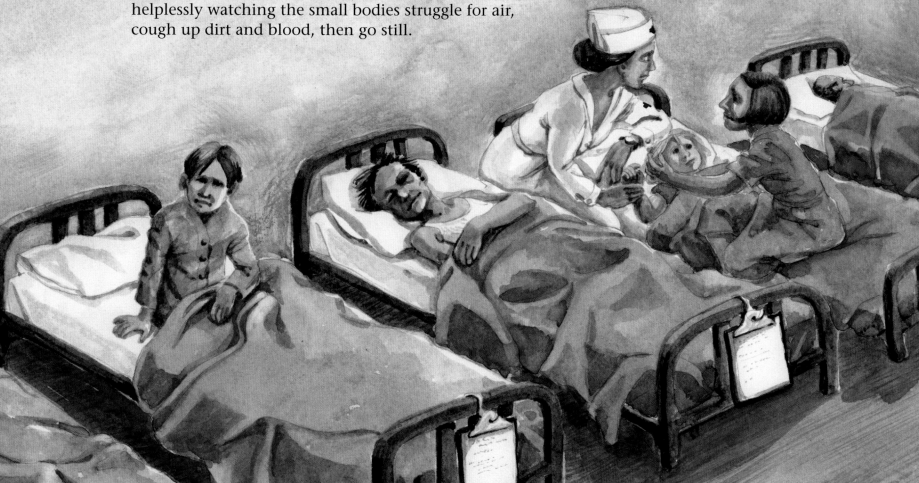

April 14, 1935—Black Sunday

I'm a store clerk on my day off.
The morning started beautifully clear.
I hopped into my Ford Model T
and drove off to visit my favorite gal.

We were having a pleasant picnic near a creek
when suddenly we heard the strange sound
of thousands of terrified birds screaming overhead,
as if being chased by a horrible beast.

To the north, we saw a tall, dark cloud
rolling toward us like boiling black smoke.

I pushed that old Flivver as hard as it would go,
but that howling, devil storm caught up to us.
The sky turned black as ink, except for
blue sparks of electricity snapping all around.
Even with the headlights on, I could not see the road.
The howling wind rocked us like a mad monster
and shoved us into a ditch.

Now I know why they call it a "black blizzard."

1936—Oklahoma

I am a mother with nine children.
Today we left the old home place
where every one of them was born,
where laughter and fiddle playing used to fill the air.

We tried to stay, but what little crops did come up
got whipped and burned and buried in dust
or eaten by the 'hoppers or the rabbits.
The bank took the house, the tractor, and the cow
on account of us not being able to pay back the loans.

We've packed everything we own, though it be not much,
into this old truck and are heading down Route 66.
We've heard there is no drouth in California,
where crops are lush and green.
There is plenty of work for everyone, and
an honest man can earn a day's pay.

God willing, we'll be there soon.

1937—Bakersville, California

I am Dorothea Lange, photographer for
the U.S. Farm Security Agency,
commissioned to take pictures of
the people affected by the Dust Bowl.

I came upon this camp of refugees.
The locals call them Okies,
no matter from whence they come.

The hunger and poverty is unspeakable.
With their ribs showing through,
they live on cornbread and red beans.

They came with dreams of jobs,
but there is only work for
a few of them, and state troopers
often turn the rest back with guns.

Some play music to pass the time.
It brings joy for the moment,
but nothing can remove the pain
from a mother's weary eyes.

1937—Texas Panhandle

I am a lonesome hobo, riding the rails,
looking for work wherever I can,
staying at a different Hooverville every night.

The train passes through one miserable town
after another—once thriving communities
that are now ghost towns buried in dust.

One year I saw hordes of hungry grasshoppers
devouring everything in sight, even bark off the posts.
'Nother year I saw a million jackrabbits
swarming over the land eating every green twig.

The cattle in the fields have long since
shriveled up to skin and bones;
most were bought and killed by the government.

Children tend their kitchen gardens
by toting water from the windmills.
The sight brings tears to my eyes for it
reminds me of my own family so far away.

1938—Kansas

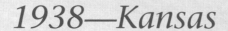

I am a worker for the Civilian Conservation Corps
formed by the U.S. government to help folks
caught in this never-ending drought
and this Great Depression.

President Roosevelt had a brainstorm:
plant millions of trees from Canada to the Rio Grande
as a shelter belt against the powerful winds
that scream across the barren fields
and carry tons and tons of topsoil away.

I don't think anything can stop this wind,
this dust, this heat, and this misery,
but I sure am thankful for the work.

1939—Texas Panhandle

I am Hugh Hammond Bennett,
director of the Soil Conservation Agency.

For years I tried to get the U.S. government
to encourage farmers to use anti-erosion measures.
No one listened until a massive dust storm
blew all the way to Washington, D.C.,
and through the windows of the Capitol.
Congress swiftly allocated money
to help farmers save the soil.

Farmers were shown a better way to till the ground,
using contours and deep chisel plowing.
They were encouraged to plant native grasses
in the fallow fields to fight the blowing wind.

By the end of last year, soil erosion
had been reduced by sixty-five percent.

Even so, there are still few crops.
What we need does not come from man.

1940—New Mexico

I am nine years old and
have never seen a good soaking rain.

A few minutes ago, I smelled something strange
and saw scary dark clouds on the horizon.
I thought it was another black roller
so I ran to tell Mama, who was
standing on the front porch.

As Papa hurried home from the fields,
the air turned cool and the wind picked up.

"Aren't you going inside?" I asked Papa.

"No, *niña,* this is one storm I want to see," he said
as the first fat raindrops hit the roof.

The rain is loud as hammers, but we haven't gone inside.
Mama and Papa are hugging each other.

"At last," Mama whispers. "At last."

Historical Note

The largest environmental catastrophe in American history took place from 1931 to 1940 during a prolonged drought on the Great Plains. The most drastically affected area included western Kansas, southeastern Colorado, northeastern New Mexico, a small part of southwestern Nebraska, and the panhandles of Texas and Oklahoma. This one-hundred-million-square-mile area became known as the "Dust Bowl." Millions of tons of topsoil were blown away in immense dust storms. Thousands of farmers lost their livelihood, their livestock, and their homes. Yet, the drought itself was not the only cause of this ecological tragedy. It was a man-made disaster that took years to develop.

For hundreds of years, the semi-arid Great Plains received an average of about fourteen inches of rain annually, with recurring cycles of wet and drought. The wind blew fiercely, at times reaching hurricane force. Native grasses such as bluestem, buffalo turf, and grama developed long roots to reach the moisture deep underground. These roots held the top layer of soil together, forming sod. Huge herds of buffalo (American bison) flourished on these grasses, multiplying until they numbered about thirty million. Droughts came and went and the winds blew, but as long as the grass roots held the sod in place, life carried on.

This changed with the arrival of American settlers. Early explorers reported that the plains were not suitable for farming and dubbed the area the "Great American Desert." But as the population grew, the demand for farmland increased. To encourage settlement, Congress passed the Homestead Act of 1862 and the Desert Land Act of 1877, which opened up millions of acres of public lands and Indian lands. The first settlers received 160-acre plots in exchange for building a dwelling and farming for five years. Some of the land was given away in large "land rushes" or "land grabs," where thousands of individuals lined up, then on signal rushed onto the plains to stake claims. The new settlers were called "homesteaders," "nesters," "sodbusters," or "sooners" and "boomers" in Oklahoma. With few trees for lumber, most of the homesteaders made houses out of sod blocks. "Dugouts" were houses that extended partially below ground.

In 1909, the Enlarged Homestead Act opened up marginal lands that were considered too dry for most farming. The homesteaders received 640 acres. The government encouraged people to come and often provided free train passage. Most people believed that when you plowed an area, that would cause rain to come. This philosophy of "rain follows the plow" beguiled farmers to move into the drier regions.

The semi-arid Plains entered a wet cycle from 1915 to 1930. When World War I (the Great War) started in 1914, the demand for wheat in war-torn Europe increased. The U.S. government urged Plains farmers to grow wheat, guaranteeing they would get at least $2.00 a bushel. The motto became "Wheat will win the war!" Farmers did so well that many took out bank loans to build new houses and buy new farming equipment. Entire towns sprang up to serve the needs of the prosperous agricultural communities.

New farm equipment inventions such as gasoline-powered tractors, harvesters, thrashers, and combines replaced mules and horse-drawn equipment, allowing the farmer to cultivate more fields with less labor. But by the late 1920s, the Great War was over and European nations were growing their own wheat again. This caused a worldwide oversupply of wheat and a drop in prices. By late 1930, the price had plummeted to twenty-four cents per bushel. Many farmers actually lost money on their crops.

Even though Plains farmers raised "bumper" crops, no one would buy the wheat. Since the silos were still full from the previous year, some farmers dumped their unsold grain on the side of the road. Farmers plowed up even more grass lands in an effort to grow more wheat to make more money. Some farmers let their fields go fallow (unplanted) rather than work so hard and get nothing.

Without warning, in October 1929, the most devastating economic disaster in American history—the Great Depression—started with the crash of the stock market. Almost overnight investors lost all their money. Many banks also lost their money, forcing them to close. Customers who had placed their life savings in the banks lost everything. When worried citizens gathered to withdraw their money, it was called a "bank run." In 1930, 256 banks failed, but by 193 he number had risen to 2,294. By 1931, twelve million peo-le were out of work—25 percent of the work force.

Then, in the summer of 1931, the unthinkable happened n the Great Plains: the rain stopped and the region entered severe nine-year drought. Wheat crops withered and died. low there were millions of acres of unplanted fields with no lant roots to hold the sod together. Under the scorching sun, le topsoil dried up and became loose. Strong winds lifted up lis soil and formed large dust storms (dusters), their color epending on which region they came from. Storms carrying lack soil were called "black blizzards" or "black rollers." Dur-ng a dust storm, it became so dark that the chickens would oost. Sometimes a storm was so strong that it reached the ast Coast and blew dust into the Atlantic Ocean. On Black unday, April 14, 1935, the largest dust storm in American istory rolled in from the northern plains, measuring two undred miles across and two thousand feet high. Its winds loved sixty-five miles per hour, and in its path, the tempera-ures dropped twenty-five degrees in an hour.

During storms, dust got into homes, businesses, schools, cars, ood, and clothing. The blowing dirt felt like abrasive sandpa-er against the skin and irritated the eyes, throat, and lungs. he Red Cross gave out free masks and set up hospitals to care or those afflicted with "dust pneumonia," a form of silicosis hat scars lung tissue and is often fatal. Colliding dust particles n the storms created static electricity, making metal items emit barks and vehicle motors to short out. Tall dust drifts buried ences, roads, and entire houses. Roofs caved in; roads became npassable. Schools and even some towns closed.

As the drought continued, dusters increased in number nd size, peaking in 1937 with 134 storms. In 1935 alone, 50 million tons of topsoil blew away. The average Dust Bowl arm lost 480 tons of topsoil per acre. Summer temperatures bared, often staying in the one hundreds for weeks at a time. treams, creeks, and some rivers dried up. Livestock starved om lack of grass; cows went blind from sand in their eyes r died from ingesting dirt. The U.S. government bought and aughtered six million pigs in 1933 and eight million cattle 1 1934. Any edible meat was given away to the needy.

Pests such as grasshoppers and rabbits invaded the rought area. The hungry grasshoppers ate everything green or woody. The invasion of 1937 numbered fourteen million grasshoppers per square mile. The National Guard was called out to help combat them. Hordes of other critters such as snakes, spiders, and centipedes crawled into the sod houses to get out of the heat.

Impoverished Plains farmers could not make their loan payments so banks foreclosed on farms and auctioned off possessions. Between 1930 and 1935, there were 750,000 farm foreclosures. During that same period, approximately one million people abandoned their farms in the Dust Bowl area to look for work. More than two hundred thousand of them moved to California, but there was not enough work for all the emigrants. State police often met the farmers with guns, and billboards along Route 66 urged the farmers not to come to California. Although most of these emigrants were not from Oklahoma, they were nicknamed "Okies," which was an insult that indicated someone was poor and home-less. All combined, about 2.5 million people moved out of all the Plains states. This became the largest single migration in the history of the United States.

Hugh Hammond Bennett, head of the new Soil Conser-vation Agency, believed that poor farming practices had contributed greatly to this environmental disaster. Ben-nett helped convince Congress to appropriate funds to teach farmers conservation. About twenty thousand gov-ernment-sponsored workers traveled to the Dust Bowl. Soil specialists showed farmers conservation methods such as con-tour plowing and chisel plowing. They encouraged farmers to plant drought-resistant grasses and to rotate crops to prevent the depletion of soil nutrients. To prevent an overabundance of certain products, the government paid farmers "subsidies" to not plant those crops. The government purchased much of the unusable land back. Some of these government lands are still sterile even today; others became protected National Grasslands.

In 1940, the rains returned, but even today, much of the earth has not recovered. It takes one thousand years to build one inch of fertile topsoil, yet only hours for a dust storm to blow it away. For all the suffering and pain endured over its nine years, the Dust Bowl remains one of the most tragic episodes in American history.

Glossary

Bale—A unit of bound ginned cotton. The first bale often receives a bonus.

Bumper crop—An exceedingly bountiful crop.

Bushel—A dry measurement equal to four pecks or thirty-two quarts.

CCC (Civilian Conservation Corps)—An organization formed to create jobs for the unemployed during the Great Depression. They worked on government projects such as building roads, bridges, parks, and helping farmers.

Chisel plowing—Deep plowing that brings large clumps of soil to the surface to provide a wind break.

Contour plowing—Plowing across a slope to prevent water runoff.

Drought/drouth—A long period of dry weather.

Flivver—Nickname for a Ford Model T automobile, produced between 1908 and 1927.

Great Plains—Semi-arid grasslands in the mid-Unite States, stretching from Canada to southern Texas, subd vided into the High Plains and Southern Plains.

Hooverville—Temporary campground of unemploye homeless persons, so named after President Herbe Hoover, whom many blamed for the Great Depression.

Shelter belt—A strip of plants, such as trees, whose pu pose is to reduce wind damage.

Subsidy, farm—Money given to the farmer by the gover ment in exchange for not planting certain crops.

Tommy gun—A Thompson brand submachine gun pop lar among gangsters.

XIT Ranch—Three million acres located in the Texas Pa handle, once the largest cattle ranch in the United State

Selected Bibliography

Bonnefield, Paul. *The Dust Bowl: Men, Dirt and the Depression.* Albuquerque: University of New Mexico Press, 1979.

Egan, Timothy. *The Worst Hard Time.* New York: Houghton Mifflin Co., 2006.

Hurt, R. Douglas. *The Dust Bowl: An Agricultural and Social History.* Chicago: Nelson Hall, 1981.

Gregory, James N. *American Exodus: The Dust Bowl Migration and Okie Culture in California.* New York: Oxford University Press, 1989.

McElevaine, Robert S. *The Great Depression: America, 1929-1941.* New York: Times Books, 1984.

Parfit, Michael. "The Dust Bowl." *Smithsonian* 20 (June 1989): 44-57.

Stallings, Frank L., Jr. *Black Sunday: The Great Dust Storm of April 14, 1935.* Austin: Eakin Press, 2001.

Svobida, Lawrence. *An Empire of Dust.* Caldwell: Caxton Printers, 1940.

Watkins, T. H. *The Great Depression: America in the 1930s.* Boston: Little, Brown & Co., 1993.

Worster, Donald. *Dust Bowl: The Southern Plains in the 1930s.* New York: Oxford University Press, 1979.

Related Books for Younger Readers

Connell, Kate. *Hoping for Rain: The Dust Bowl Adventures Patty and Earl Buckler.* Washington, D.C.: National Geo graphic Children's Books, 2004.

Cooper, Michael L. *Dust to Eat: Drought and Depression in th 1930s.* New York: Clarion Books, 2004.

Durbin, William. *Journal of C. J. Jackson, a Dust Bowl Migran* New York: Scholastic Inc., 2002.

Hesse, Karen. *Out of the Dust.* New York: Scholastic Inc., 199

Janke, Katelyn. *Survival in the Storm: The Dust Bowl Diary Grace Edwards.* New York: Scholastic Inc., 2002.

Levey, Richard H., and Daniel H. Franck. *Dust Bowl: The 193 Black Blizzards.* New York: Bearport Publishing Co., 2005.

Marrin, Albert. *Years of Dust.* New York: Dutton Children Books, 2009.

Porter, Tracey. *Treasures in the Dust.* New York: HarperColli Children's Books, 1997.

Stanley, Jerry. *Children of the Dust Bowl: The True Story of th School at Weedpatch Camp.* New York: Crown Publishin Co., 1992.

Turner, Ann, and Robert Barrett. *Dust for Dinner.* New Yor HarperTrophy, 1995.